Walki~~ng the~~ North York Moors

compiled by

The Ramblers' Association
(North Yorkshire and South Durham Area)

Dalesman Books
1993

The Dalesman Publishing Company Ltd.
Clapham, via Lancaster LA2 8EB

First published 1973
Second edition 1989
Reprinted 1993

ISBN: 0 85206 969 3

Cover drawing of Roseberry Topping by Bernard Fearnley
Maps by R. Gibbs

Printed by Lavenham Press, Lavenham, Suffolk

Contents

Introduction

THIS book has been prepared by the North Yorkshire and South Durham Area of the Ramblers' Association and contains circular walks varying in length from five-and-a-half miles to ten miles. In writing the book the aim has been to describe each walk with sufficient precision to enable it to be followed without a detailed map. Nevertheless, it is recommended that the Ordnance Survey Tourist Map of the North York Moors should also be carried, since it shows additional features of the landscape and also will be useful for getting you to the starting points of the walks.

Public Transport
Details of public transport services are shown when available. However, it must be emphasised that on some bus routes there is only a minimal service and walkers should consider carefully whether they can complete the walk without missing the only homeward bus. The main bus operator is United Automobile Services of Grange Road, Darlington, Co. Durham DL1 5NL. (Tel: Darlington 465252). Information on other operators is given against the individual walks.

Footwear and Clothing
For all the walks the need to wear adequate footwear and to carry waterproof clothing must be emphasised. Some of the walks are on rough footpaths, possibly on moorland, and it is easy to sprain an ankle if one's shoes are too lightweight. High heels are most unsuitable. In addition, it may be fine weather when you start the walk, but the weather may change, hence the need for waterproof clothing.

Respect the Countryside
Most of the walks follow established public rights of way, the main exception being in certain forest areas, where the Forestry Commission permits the use of forest tracks. When walking in forestry be careful not to start a fire. Also please remember, when crossing farmland, that this is the source of someone's livelihood, and to take particular care not to trample on crops and do not leave gates open, allowing cattle to stray from one field to another. Furthermore, if you have a dog, please keep it under control.

Problems of Routefinding

Finally, although care has been taken to ensure the accuracy of the descriptions of the walks, problems of routefinding may still arise as a result of changes in the countryside. If you experience problems in following one of the walks, or notice any changes since the book was written, please let us know about it, so that the book can be corrected when reprinted. Address any correspondence to: Dr. G.L. Cain, Ramblers' Association, 3 Stainsby Gate, Thornaby, Stockton on Tees, Cleveland TS17 9AQ.

The Hole of Horcum

Starting Point: Car park near the A.A. 'phone box, ½ mile south of the Saltergate Inn on the A169 Whitby to Pickering road, G.R. 853937.

Public Transport: Bus service 92, York-Malton-Pickering-Whitby operated by York City & District (Tel: York 624161) passes the starting point.

Distance: 5½ or 7 miles.

FROM the car park, cross over the main road and turn right along a path which follows the edge of the Hole of Horcum. As you approach the angle of the hairpin bend, pass to the left of a concrete barrier and keep straight ahead, passing through a gate and continuing along a wide stony track. This track takes you along the northern edge of the Hole of Horcum and continues over heather moorland past Seavy

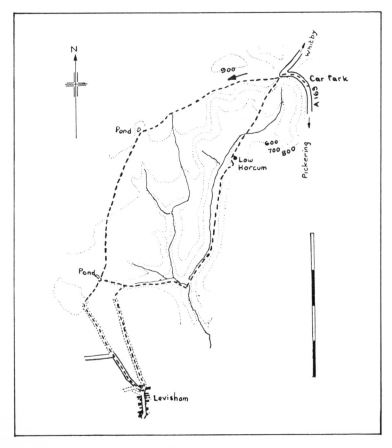

Pond to reach Dundale Pond, which is two miles from the road. If you wish to shorten the walk, turn sharply left on to a wide grassy track which descends into a shallow valley, then continue as described in the next paragraph. Otherwise use the path signposted 'R.A. Extension Route which goes diagonally to the right and leads to a gate and stile at the end of an enclosed lane. Continue along the lane and keep straight ahead to reach the Horse Shoe Inn at Levisham and return by the lane on the other side of the inn. Cross over the stile at the far end of the lane and bear right down the hillside to join the path from Dundale Pond.

The path from Dundale Pond continues alongside a tree-lined ravine and, if you keep to the right of the streamlet at the bottom, you will come to a wooden footpath signpost. Turn left here, cross over the steamlet and the footbridge over Levisham Beck, which is very narrow at this point. Continue along the path between the beck and the wall, then walk over the fields to Low Horcum Farm, keeping halfway between the beck and the wood on your right. Pass immediately to the left of the farm and follow a wide grassy track to a stile and gate in the valley bottom. The track then continues straight ahead and climbs up the hillside to join the main road at the hairpin bend. Turn right to reach the car park.

Troutsdale

Starting Point: Car park, a quarter of a mile north of Cockmoor Hall, on the road which runs northwards into Troutsdale from Snainton on the A170, G.R. 914868.

Distance: 9 miles.

FOLLOW the rough road, which starts at the car park, then passes through a gate and continues alongside part of Wykeham Forest. After passing a forest nursery, a bend in a motor road is reached. Continue forward along this road for about a mile as far as the crossroads at Bakers Warren, where there is a car park and viewpoint, then turn left and follow a steep winding road down to Troutsdale Beck and the Troutsdale road.

Turn left and walk along the road to the first farm, Troutsdale Low Hall, where you turn right near a wooden garage on to a narrow road, signposted 'Unsuitable for motors', which leads to Freeze Gill Farm. Behind the farm a broad sunken track slants steeply upwards to the right through the gorse bushes and then passes through woodland,

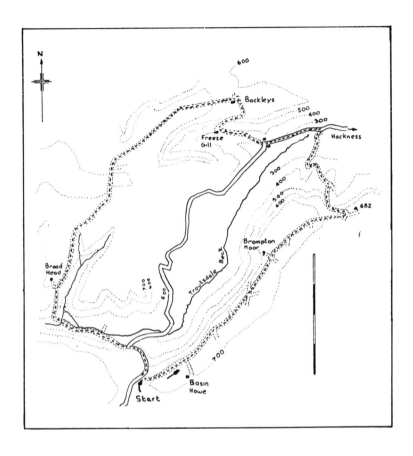

before continuing to Backleys Farm. Walk past the right-hand side of the farmhouse, turn left and pass behind all the farm buildings, continuing alongside the right-hand side of a wall to a gate marked 'Right of Way'. On the other side of this, keep straight ahead and follow a wire fence to reach a stile on to a forest road.

Turn left and follow the road, ignoring all side tracks until you reach a clearing on the left with a view into Troutsdale. The road, which you have been following, turns right to Broad Head Farm, just around the corner, but you must turn left at the clearing and follow another rough road down into Troutsdale. On reaching the motor road, keep straight on and climb the hill back to the car park.

Hackness and Broxa

Starting Point: Near Hackness Church at the end of the road signposted 'Low Dales and High Dales only', G.R. 967906.

Public Transport: Bus service 111, Scarborough-Bickley operated by Scarborough and District (Tel: Scarborough 375463) on Thursdays and Saturdays stops at Hackness Post Office, which is just past the start of the walk.

Distance: 9½ miles.

WALK along the signposted road for about a mile as far as the point where Lowdales Beck emerges from a culvert under the road and

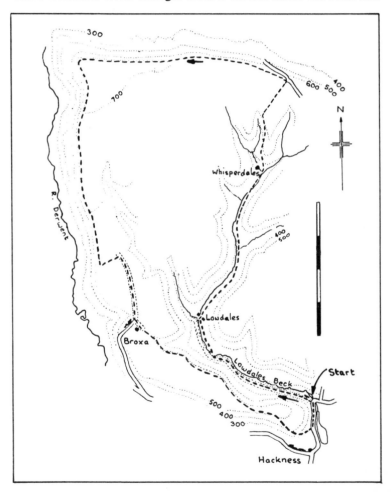

flows under a footbridge on your right. Cross the footbridge and continue over a field to Lowdales Farm, visible ahead. Pass to the left of the farmhouse and walk along a wide track between the house and the farm outbuildings, proceeding over a footbridge and then bearing right over another footbridge. The track then goes through a gate and continues as a field road for 1¼ miles to Whisperdales Farm. At the farm proceed along the farm track on the outside of a wire fence; it swings round to the right and then the left and ascends a spur between two minor tributary valleys. The track soon enters a forest and, if you keep straight ahead, you will reach a 'T' junction near the gravel-surfaced car park at Reasty Bank Top.

Turn left and follow a broad forest track along the edge of the north-facing escarpment above Harwood Dale. After about a mile, the track swings to the left into deep forest, but your route keeps to the escarpment along a slightly narrower track. Three-quarters of a mile later, this track turns sharply to the left at a point where there is a good view over to Langdale Rigg, then continues southwards. Now keep walking southwards and, when the track turns left after about 1½ miles, keep straight ahead still in a southerly direction. When you reach farmland, turn left along the forest edge then right along the road to Broxa. After passing a bungalow on your left at the edge of the village, turn left along a farm road beside a large corrugated-sheeted barn. Go past the farmhouse, cross over the stile ahead of you at the end of the road, walk diagonally across the field to the far left-hand corner and continue along the top edge of a wood. Eventually you pass through a gate in the centre of a stone wall across the top of the ridge. Now follow a broad track for a short distance through the waste land, then bear right towards the wood and follow the edge of the wood to a gate set back on your right. Cross over the stile near the gate and follow a wide track which descends through the wood. When you reach a junction with a similar track, bear left to reach the road at the bottom, then turn left to return to your starting point.

Ravenscar and Hayburn Wyke

Starting Point: Roadside car park near the Raven Hall Hotel, Ravenscar, G.R. 980015.

Public Transport: Bus service 115, Scarborough-Cloughton-Ravenscar operated by Scarborough and District (Tel: Scarborough 375463) on Tuesdays, Thursdays and Saturdays.

Distance: 8½ miles.

FROM the car park, follow the road round to the right past the entrance to the Raven Hall Hotel and the bus stopping place, then turn left along a rough road signposted 'Cleveland Way'. Turn right at the cliff edge and follow the cliff top path for 3½ miles to Hayburn Wyke, where it descends to a substantial footbridge over Hayburn Beck which flows over a waterfall on to the beach. To visit the beach, turn left at the footbridge, otherwise continue straight ahead along a path which ascends through a wood and passes to the right of a Nature Reserve sign. Continue until the broad main path turns sharply to the left and you can see the stone steps on another path ahead of you. About 60 feet before the steps, turn right along a narrow path which descends to a footbridge over Hayburn Beck and then turns left. Now follow the path upstream keeping close to the beck; eventually it gradually diverges from the beck and leads to the top of the wood. Proceed until you reach a farm track.

Turn left and walk to the end of the track, then bear right along a tarred road. At the next junction, go along the road described as 'Unsuitable for motors', passing Plane Tree Cottages to reach Plane Tree Farm, where you pass to the right of all the buildings and continue straight ahead to White Hall Farm. At this farm, keep straight ahead along a wide rough enclosed track. At the end of the enclosed section, it goes through a gate and becomes a field road with a wall on its right-hand side. Keep straight ahead, passing through two more gates and, at the second gate, turn sharply to the right and follow the wall to reach the access road to Prospect House Farm just north of the farm. Turn left and walk along the road to Ravenscar Church, where you turn right to return to your starting point.

(see map on page 12)

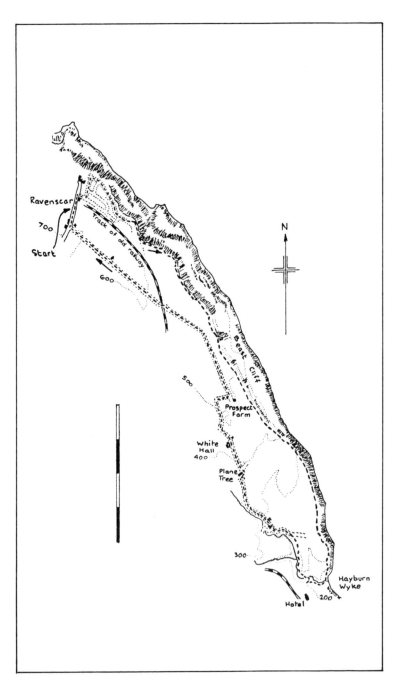

Ravenscar

700

Start

Track of old railway

600

N

500

Beast Cliff

Prospect Farm

White Hall
400

Plane Tree

300

Hayburn Wyke

200

Hotel

Hawsker Bottoms and The Riggs

Starting Point: Whitby Abbey car park, G.R. 903113.

Public Transport: Whitby can be reached by railway from Middlesbrough and by bus services from Scarborough, Middlesbrough, Guisborough and Loftus (operated by United) and also York, Malton and Pickering (operated by York City & District - Tel: York 624161).

Distance: 9 miles.

FROM the abbey car park, make for the Coastguard Station and follow the Cleveland Way coastal footpath away from Whitby. When you reach Saltwick Nab, follow the road through the caravan site and continue along the cliff path on the other side. Further on the path passes the fog signal, then goes diagonally across a field to a stile; cross over the road on the other side and continue along the outside of the boundary wall of the lighthouse and along the coast.

Take care when crossing the gullies through which streams reach the sea, since they can be slippery in wet weather. Immediately after passing the third of these since the lighthouse, turn inland along the path signposted 'Hawsker', and just before you reach the caravans, bear left on to a tarmac road and continue straight ahead through the caravan site. At the entrance to the site at the top, turn right and follow the access road, which eventually joins the Robin Hood's Bay road at a bend. Keep straight on and follow the road into High Hawsker, where it bears right in the direction of Whitby and continues to meet the A171 road near a chapel.

Cross over the main road and walk along the road through Low Hawsker, passing the ancient Hawsker Cross, which can be seen in a garden on the right at the far end of the village. The road then descends a hill, and at the bend at the bottom there is a stile on your right. Cross over the stile and the nearby beck, then ascend to another stile. On the other side of this, follow the short section of hedge on your left, then keep straight on across a large field to reach and cross over a third stile hidden away near a tall ash tree. After crossing a ditch, the path bears right over another ditch and continues uphill to a stile near a gate. Cross over the stile and walk alongside the hedge on your left to reach Stainsacre Lane. Turn left, go past Asp Lodge and turn right along a narrow road. This turns right at the house called The Riggs and, half a mile later where the road turns left downhill, you must bear slightly to the right along a track signposted Stainsacre Hall and go through a gate into a field.

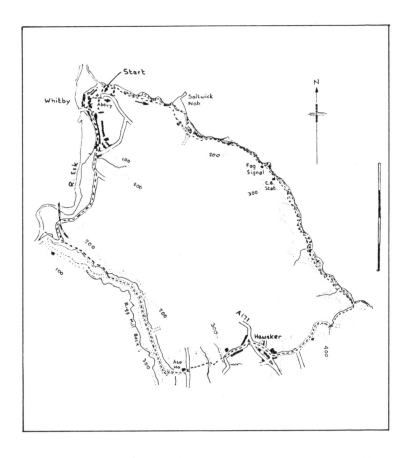

Follow the hedge on your left to a gap at the end of the field and continue on the other side beside the hedge along a hard surfaced field road which soon turns left. However, do not turn left but keep straight ahead keeping parallel to the valley on your right to reach a gate giving access to an enclosed green lane. Continue forward; the surface gradually changes and eventually you will find yourself walking along a tarmac lane. Immediately after reaching a large house on the right (Golden Grove), leave the road and bear right across a paved yard, then turn left along a narrow paved path past Waterfall Cottage. Continue along the right-hand side of stream to reach a road. Turn right and follow the road, passing high above the River Esk before dropping down to the Whitby by-pass road. Cross over this and walk down the main road to the harbour. Green Lane on the right will take you back to your starting point but is not very interesting. It is better to continue along the harbourside and then along Church Street to the bottom of the 199 steps which lead up to St. Mary's Church and the abbey car park.

Waterfalls Near Goathland

Starting Point: Mallyan Hotel opposite Goathland Parish Church, G.R. 828007.

Public Transport: The following bus services stop at the Mallyan Hotel: 95, Whitby-Goathland (operated by United on Monday to Saturday) and 92, York-Malton-Pickering-Whitby (operated by York City & District - Tel: York 624161). The walk can also be started from Goathland station.

Distance: 6½ miles.

START the walk by using the narrow signposted path from the right-hand side of the Mallyan Hotel. When you reach the West Beck, turn left and go upstream for about a quarter of a mile and, after a scramble over the rocks, Mallyan Spout will be seen cascading over the moss-covered cliff on your left. Retrace your steps to the foot of the path from the hotel, then walk downstream and cross over a stile. A well-trodden path follows the woodside above West Beck, eventually descending steeply to the beck and leading to a stone cottage, called Incline Cottage. Turn left at the cottage and follow a rough-surfaced track which soon turns right through a gate, thereby reaching the Birch Hall Inn at Beck Hole.

Cross the bridge over the Eller Beck and turn sharply to the right at the letter box along a path signposted 'Thomason Foss Only'. The path passes to the right of a cottage and immediately forks. The right-hand fork makes a detour to Thomason Foss, a distance of about a mile there and back. This path climbs up to the railway fence, then descends to the beck and continues to the waterfall, where it terminates. Return to the fork at the cottage and continue round the back of the cottage to reach the road near the railway bridge. On the far side of the bridge, turn right along the rough road to Hill Farm. As you approach the farm leave the road and walk alongside the wall on your right, continuing along a grassy track towards the left-hand side of the next farm, called Lins Farm. On the other side of this farm, the track follows a wall and reaches a seat, beyond which a narrower path continues part way up the hillside above the Eller Beck. A waterfall called Water Ark Foss is down below, somewhat hidden when the surrounding trees are in leaf.

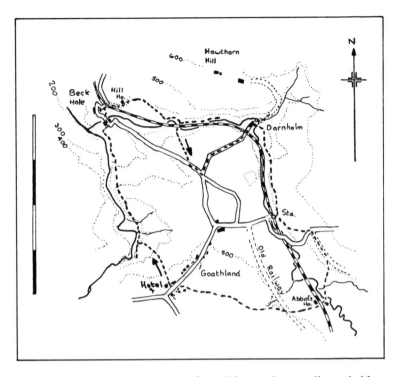

Continue forward towards a footbridge under a railway bridge. Another small waterfall, Walk Mill Foss, is about quarter of a mile upstream and can be visited by turning left before the footbridge and following the railway boundary wall, then the bank of the beck. Return by the same route. Otherwise, cross over the footbridge, ascend the steps to the stile at the top, then bear left and pass between two old stone gateposts. A well-defined path continues to the Goathland to Beck Hole road, where you turn left and follow the road to a crossroads, before turning left along the road through Darnholm.

Continue over the railway bridge and proceed until you nearly reach a stone cottage on the left, then turn right along a narrow path beside a wooden fence. On the other side of the footbridge, follow a grassy path which swings round to the right and comes alongside the boundary wall of the railway near a brick bridge. The path then follows the wall to a point near Goathland Station.

From the station, walk uphill alongside the railway boundary wall, using a wide grassy track which turns left near a seat and heads for the left-hand end of the row of cottages. At the cottages, turn right and follow the garden wall, then bear left to join a road. The route continues along a narrow lane, which is slightly uphill of the notice to bus drivers on the opposite side of the road. There is a wall on your right and, when it bears away from the lane, leave the lane and walk beside it. When the wall turns right towards a farm, keep straight ahead and cross over a stile to the right of a marshy hollow.

Walk down the hollow, continuing over a stone slab footbridge and through a gate to the right of a bungalow. Cross another footbridge, pass to the right of a farm, then go under the railway bridge and follow a farm road uphill. When this turns right at what might be described as a crossroads, go straight across into the field opposite. Walk alongside the hedge on your left, cross over a stile, turn right and cross over a stone stile near a ditch. Turn left and follow the hedge and then a wire fence to reach another stile. Keep straight ahead along the edge of two more fields. Finally, go through a gate in a stone wall and keep straight on along a wide track to reach the church near the Mallyan Hotel.

Lower Rosedale

Starting Point: Parking place near the steep hill notice at the top of Rosedale Chimney Bank, 1 mile south of Rosedale Abbey on the road from Hutton-le-Hole to Rosedale Abbey, G.R. 720945.

Distance: 9 miles.

START by walking along the wide grassy track, which leaves the road on the right-hand side of the underground reservoir opposite the steep hill sign. As you approach Ana Cross, leave the track and head for the cross, continuing on the other side in a southerly direction along the path indentified by a stone cairn and then a wide track bulldozed through the heather. Two miles south of the cross there is a gate across the track; go through this and continue down a lane which descends into Lastingham. If you would like to explore the village and visit its interesting old church, turn right at the junction at the bottom, otherwise turn left along the road to Cropton. Follow this for about a mile until it turns sharply to the right, then turn left along a narrow lane.

Eventually the lane descends towards High Askew and turns right to reach a gate. Do not go through this but turn left and walk alongside a wire fence which forms the boundary between a wood and the open

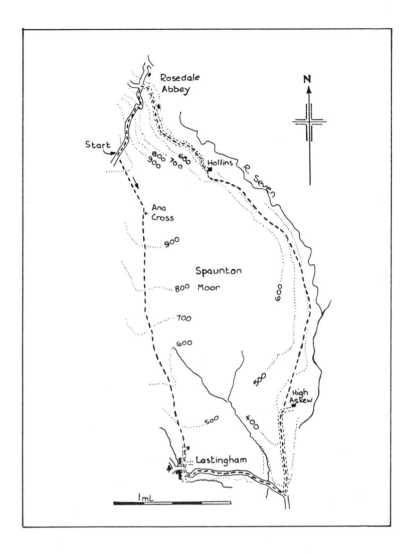

moor. Continue alongside a stone wall and, when this turns sharply to the right, keep straight ahead through the bracken, passing just to the right a birch tree. The path passes two more birch trees and, just after this, a very well-defined path leads up the dale, more or less parallel to the River Seven. The way is straightforward until you come to the end of a stone wall, where you must bear slightly to the left, since the path continues parallel to the wall but slightly uphill from it.

One mile later the path descends to the access road to Hollins

Farm, where you turn left and follow the road to its junction with the road up Rosedale Chimney Bank near the White Horse Farm Hotel. Ascend the hill back to your starting point.

Rosedale Ironstone Railway

Starting Point: Parking place near the steep hill notice at the top of Rosedale Chimney Bank, 1 mile south of Rosedale Abbey on the road from Hutton-le-hole to Rosedale Abbey, G.R. 720945.

Distance: 11 miles.

THIS walk follows the track of the former Rosedale ironstone railway, which was used to transfer iron ore from the Rosedale mines to the iron works of Middlesbrough and other places. Although it is not officially designated as a right of way, we believe that the farmers and landowners in Rosedale have no objection to walkers using the railway.

Commence the walk by following the road down Rosedale Chimney Bank until you reach the White Horse Farm Hotel, then turn left along the road signposted 'Thorgill Only'. One mile later, just before a sharp left-hand bend is reached, turn right down a short farm road to Low Thorgill Farm. This passes between a group of farm buildings and turns right towards the farmhouse. Continue through the gate on the right with the public footpath sign, then walk diagonally to the left and cross a footbridge over the River Seven. Bear left along a paved trod; after the first field, the stones are buried under the turf but a distinct path continues uphill to a gap in a hedge. Continue to a gate and kissing gate at the top of the next field, then bear left along a wide track which leads to a road near a terrace of cottages, originally built for workers in the old ironstone mining industry.

Take the track immediately opposite which ascends to the site of the Rosedale goods station at the eastern terminus of the former Rosedale ironstone railway. On the way you will pass a white house, once the 'Depot Cottage', and the ruins of the coal depot. At the top of the bank, go through a gate, walk past the former goods shed (surrounded by corrugated iron lean-to buildings) and past the left-hand side of the ruined cottages of Low Baring to reach the trackbed of the old railway. From now on the route is straightforward along the

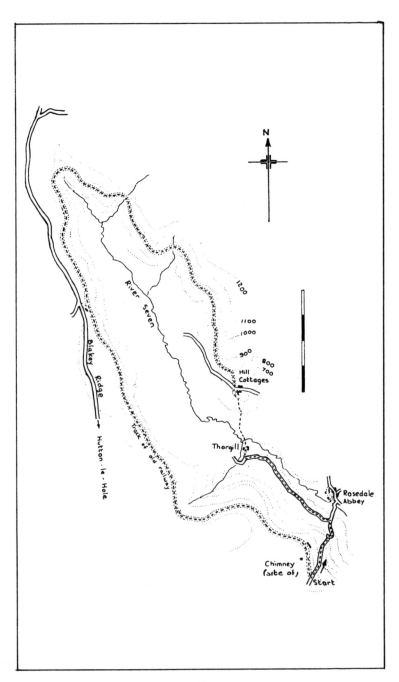

N

River Seven

Blakey Ridge

Hutton-le-Hole

Track of old railway

1200
1100
1000
900
800
700

Hill Cottages

Thorgill

Rosedale Abbey

Chimney (site of)

Start

railway track for 8½ miles around the head of Rosedale and back to your starting point near the western terminus of the railway at Bank Top. Within the first mile you will see evidence of the ironstone mining and will pass the remains of the 'Old Kilns' and 'New Kilns', used to roast the ore and reduce its weight before transit.

Upper Farndale

Starting Point: Junction of the road from Castleton to Hutton-le-Hole and the road into Farndale via Blakey Bank, ½ mile south of the Lion Inn, G.R. 684989.

Distance: 11 miles.

START by walking about 20 yards down the road into Farndale, then turn right and continue along the old railway track for 3 miles until you reach the point where a wide cinder track on your right descends to the head of Westerdale. Turn left along the grassy bridleway opposite the cinder track; the path soon passes some grouse shooting butts, which are at first on your right and then on your left. After the last butt the route becomes less obvious and you should look for a depression in the ground on your left and three prominent trees. The route continues straight ahead parallel to the right-hand side of the depression and passes about 70 feet to the right of the first tree and then through a line of fence posts. Now descend to the developing stream gully ahead of you and follow the obvious narrow path on its left-hand side until the streamlet passes through a fallen section of stone wall and enters a wooded ravine.

Beyond the wall the route of the bridleway is identified by the wide boggy depression to the right of the streamlet; avoid the initial boggy section by following the narrow path on its left-hand side and continue on the left-hand side when the depression swings to the right away from the wood and continues parallel to the wall on the uphill side of you. This leads you to a gap in a stone wall, where there was once a gate. The bridleway continues straight ahead in a reed-filled hollow; follow it down to the corner of a stone wall, then head down a grassy hollow to a gate opposite Esk House Farm giving access to the lane on the east side of Farndale.

Turn left and follow the lane to the 'Feversham Arms' at Church

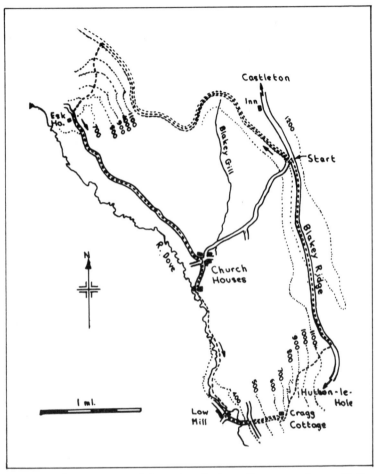

Houses, where you turn right and walk along the narrow lane with the 'No Through Road' sign. This leads to High Mill, where you pass between the buildings and continue along a field path, which is known as the 'Daffodil Walk' because in April it passes through a sea of daffodils. The path crosses a bridge over a little stream, goes through a gate in a wall and leads to a stile on the edge of a small wood near the River Dove. Note: make sure that you do not go through the wicket gate, which is slightly uphill from the stile. On the other side of the stile, a pleasant path follows the riverbank towards the village of Low Mill, where there is a substantial footbridge over the river. Cross over the bridge and ascend to the road.

Turn left into the village and then turn left by the Methodist Church to descend back to the valley bottom and ultimately reach a 'T' junction of metalled roads. Continue along a rough farm track, signposted 'Footpath to Rosedale', which starts at the junction and ascends the daleside to Cragg Cottage. Go through the gate to the right of the outbuildings at the cottage, then through another gate. Your path now follows the wall behind the cottage, turns right and, almost immediately afterwards, goes diagonally uphill to the left. Ascend through the bracken to a stile in a wall and continue diagonally uphill on the other side. After passing through a gate near a clump of trees, the path levels out and then becomes a sunken track which eventually swings round to the right and passes to the left of the quarry spoil heaps. This last section is waterlogged and an alternative path has been worn through the bracken to the left of it. This takes you to a line of shooting butts, which are followed to reach the Hutton-le-Hole to Castleton road. Turn left and walk along the road for two miles back to the starting point.

Westerdale

Starting Point: Centre of Westerdale village, G.R. 666058.

Distance: 9½ miles.

LEAVE Westerdale village near the church by a lane which starts at the telephone kiosk and passes to the right of the public conveniences. Proceed along this winding road past the Youth Hostel and Hall Farm, across the River Esk, through a gate in a wall and straight on to another gate at the edge of the moor. Go through this and turn left along the road to New House. At the bend just before the farm, pass through the second of two gates on the left and keep straight ahead across the first field. Cross Stockdale Beck by a footbridge in the far left-hand corner of the next field, continue along the River Esk and cross over the remains of a wall, followed by a stone step stile to the left of an electricity pole. Keep straight on across the next field, cross over a farm access road, climb over the stile on the far side of the field and head for Wood End Farm, visible in front of you.

When you approach Wood End Farm, go through the gate on the right, then walk behind the farmhouse and continue straight ahead through the gate into the stackyard. Cross over a stone step stile, followed by a footbridge, then bear left to reach and cross a footbridge

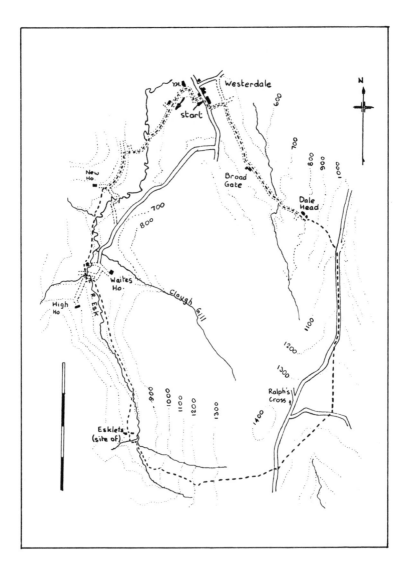

near a ford. Now turn right and follow the footpath signposted
'Footpath to Farndale'; this well-trodden path continues up the
valley, more or less parallel to the river, and about a mile later crosses
the river by means of a footbridge. Continue upstream, cross a stile in
a wall after which the path slants away from the river and goes slightly
uphill. Pass through two stone gateposts into a small field, follow the
wall on your right, then bear left and leave the field through a gap in a

wall. Keep straight ahead past the stone rubble which marks the site of the former farmhouse of Esklets, then continue along the wide enclosed track which used to be the access road.

The track soon crosses a stream, then goes uphill and turns sharply to the right. At this point, turn left and walk over the grass to a white-topped marker post, then cross over the stream. Now follow the wall on your right, go through the old stone gateposts into the next field and immediately turn left. Continue uphill, following the wall on your left, then bear slightly to the right through a gap in a wall and proceed to two old stone gateposts in another wall. The path then continues over heather moor to reach the road over Blakey Ridge at the Margery Bradley Stone. Cross the road, then bear left along a narrow path in the heather, leading over the head of Rosedale to reach the Castleton to Rosedale Road at White Cross (sometimes called Fat Betty).

Cross straight over the road and follow another narrow path which starts just to the right of the cross and follows the parish boundary stones to reach the road over Castleton Rigg. Continue forward along the road for about three quarters of a mile until you reach the point where it is joined by a narrow road which descends steeply into Danby Dale on your right-hand side. Over on your left is a linear earthwork called High Stone Dike, surmounted by a boundary stone, and about 40 feet beyond this a narrow path goes diagonally over the moor. Continue along this path; it soon becomes a distinct sunken track and descends to a gate in a wall at Dale Head Farm. Go through the gate, then turn left at the sycamore tree opposite you and go through the gap between the stone cart shed and the barn. Behind the barn is a wide track, which forks opposite the farmhouse. Follow the right-hand fork to two gates side by side, then go through the right-hand gate and continue alongside the wall on your left.

Descend through a wood and, after crossing Tower Beck, go through a gate into a field. Keep straight on across the field, then head for the gate in the wall opposite you. On the other side of the gate a distinct track leads to Broad Gate Farm, beyond which it continues as a tarred road. About half a mile from the farm a crossroads is reached and you should turn left into Westerdale village.

Egton Banks and Ugthorpe

Starting Point: Lay-by at Barton Howl near Egton on the A171 Whitby to Middlesbrough moor road, G.R. 803083.

Public Transport: Most journeys on United bus route 93, Stockton-Middlesbrough-Whitby-Scarborough, pass the starting point. Some journeys are routed via Egton Cross and by-pass the starting point, but pass Moor Side Farm which is on the route of the walk.

Distance: 6 miles or 9 miles.

WALK a short distance along the main road in the Guisborough direction and turn left on to a minor road. At the crossroads, turn left and, about a quarter of a mile later, turn right along the access road to Moor Side Farm. Pass in front of the farm buildings and proceed along the continuation of the access road. At the next farm (Howe House), go through the gate between the corrugated iron garage and the stone farm buildings, then turn right. Follow the wire fence to the corner of the field, then swing to the left and walk alongside a ditch and wire fence until the fence turns sharply to the right. Now cross over the ditch and follow the continuation of the wire fence and then a hedge, finally turning right along a wide enclosed track leading to Westonby House.

Continue along the farm access road, turn left along the Glaisdale road, then turn right after a short distance along the farm road to Thorn Hill. Go through the gate across the road at the farm, followed by a wicket gate into the field on your left. Walk beside the cattle pen, then head for a stone pillar followed by some hawthorns which form part of an old hedge. Turn sharply to the left and follow the far side of the old hedge down to about 50 feet from the stream at the bottom, where you turn right and walk between the trees parallel to the stream. Cross over the footbridge spanning Stonegate Beck, follow the hedge on your right to reach Hall Park Farm and then turn left along the farm access road.

Walk along the road for about half a mile until it crosses over a ditch through a gate in a fence, then continue for a short distance until it turn sharply to the left. Now cross over the stile in the wooden fence on your right, turn left and follow a hedge to a gap between the hedge and a wall near the end of the field. Go through the gap into the next field and follow the wall; almost immediately it bends to the right, but you must stay in the same field and walk along the edge of the field beside a wall and pass through a gate in the wire fence at the far end. Walk straight across the next field, go through a gate in a wall, bear right

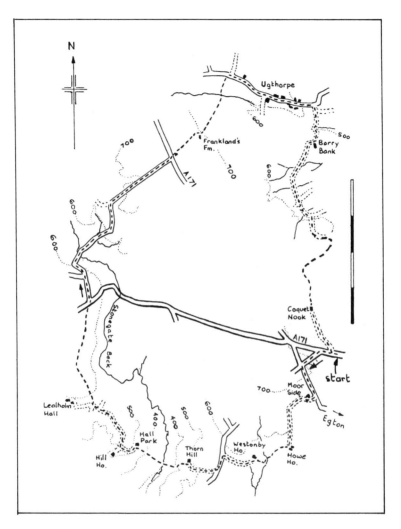

alongside a wire fence and go through a gate on to rough moorland. If you look in the direction of Stonegate Farm with the slate roof, you will see the next gate. Follow the path through it, then walk alongside the wall to reach the Lealholm road.

For a shorter six mile walk, turn right here and keep straight on to the A171, then continue forward to reach your starting point. Otherwise continue along the Guisborough road opposite you and follow it to the A171. High Park Farm is now in front of you; go through the farm gate, past the left-hand side of the farmhouse, then through two gates in succession. Continue past the right-hand side of the covered reservoir and diagonally across the next field, to cross over a stile near a field gate to the left of Frankland's Farm. Turn right and go through the gate by the electricity pole, then turn left and follow the hedge for two fields, continuing along a wide field track. The track crosses a ditch and then there are two stiles on the right-hand side of the track. Cross the second one, situated where the track straightens out after the bend, turn right through the gate at the top of the field and cross the next field to a gate on the road near Ugthorpe Mill.

Turn right and walk to the far end of Ugthorpe village, then turn right along a farm road by Christ Church. At Barry Bank Farm, a quarter of a mile later, turn right through a gate and follow a field road to reach Ugthorpe Grange, where you keep straight on along a tarmac road. This turn right at its junction with the rough road to Mulgrave Farm and is followed as far as the next farmhouse called Biggin House. Now go through the gate immediately opposite the house, bear left and walk alongside the field boundary to reach a gate at the top of the field. Continue straight ahead on the other side of gate; the route soon becomes indistinct and is indentified by tractor tracks in the heather. As you approach a gate on your left, the tracks swing slightly to the right and lead to a short wooden marker post beside a telephone junction box. Now look for a gate on your left with a holly bush on the other side. Go through the gate, follow the hedge n your right to the end of the field, enter the next field and immediately bear left and continue past the left-hand side of Coquet Nook Farm. Its access road takes you to your starting point.

Fryup Dale

Starting Point - Long walk: Near the Fox and Hounds Inn, Ainthorpe, on the minor road to Fryup Dale, G.R. 705077. Please do not use the inn car park. Short walk: In Little Fryup Dale at the road junction near Crossley House Farm, G.R. 711055.

Public Transport: Danby Railway Station on the Middlesbrough to Whitby line is 1 mile from the starting point (no Sunday services except in summer).

Distance: 7 or 10 miles.

FROM the Fox and Hounds Inn, walk uphill along the road, passing the tennis courts and continuing until you almost reach the crest of the

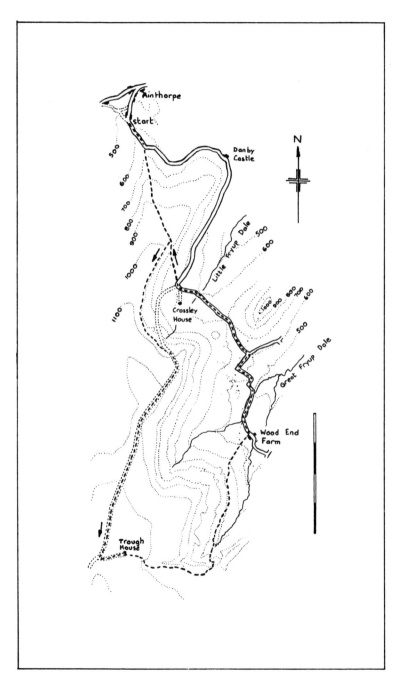

Ainthorpe

start

Danby
Castle

500

600

700

800

900

1000

1100

N

Little Fryup Dole

500

600

1000 900 800 700 600

500

Crossley
House

Great Fryup Dole

Wood End
Farm

Trough
House

hill. At this point, veer off right along the public bridleway which passes through a hollow between the gorse bushes and continues over the top of the moor. When the path starts to descend into Little Fryup Dale, turn right and follow a narrow path along the edge of the moor.

Eventually you reach the single track road which has come up from the alternative starting point in Little Fryup Dale. Walk uphill along the road for two miles, then turn left at a 'Public Bridleway' sign and follow a wide track to Trough House, a stone shooting lodge. Continue to a large cairn at the lowest point of the track and then turn left along a path which descends into Great Fryup Dale. The path crosses two small streams, then passes through a gate in a wall near a corrugated iron shed, bears slightly to the left and continues down the dale through bracken. About 300 yards later, the path passes to the left of a wall and you continue with the wall and then a wire fence on your right-hand side for three quarters of a mile. The path then passes through two gates in succession and goes down a grass field to another gate. On the other side of this, walk alongside the wire fence and head for a gate to the left of Wood End Farm, giving access to a narrow road.

Turn left and follow the road; about a quarter of a mile later it climbs steeply and turns sharply to the right at a 'T' junction with a concrete farm road. Shortly after this, the road descends and swings round to the left to a road junction with a signpost. Continue straight ahead along the Danby road; after crossing over a cattle grid, it ascends to a 'T' junction near Crossley House Farm, the alternative starting point. The path signposted 'Bridleway to Ainthorpe' which goes diagonally to the right up Danby Rigg, takes you back to Ainthorpe by the reverse of the outward route. It is also possible to follow the metalled road back past Danby Castle.

Glaisdale

Starting Point: Glaisdale Railway Station, G.R. 783056.

Public Transport: Glaisdale Station is on the Middlesbrough to Whitby railway line (no Sunday services except in summer).

Distance: 8 miles.

FROM the station yard walk down the road to near the railway bridge and then turn right over a footbridge. Follow the steps round to the left

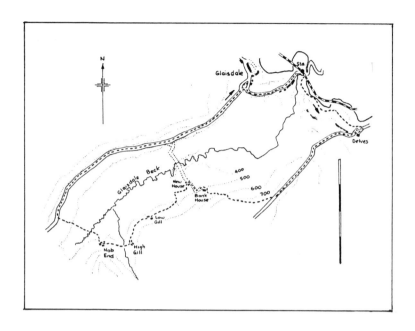

and continue through East Arncliffe Wood to reach the Rosedale
Abbey to Egton road. Turn right and walk along the road for about a
mile as far as a cattle grid. Just beyond this, veer off to the right along a
wide track which follows the edge of the forest. Continue along this
track; after passing through the forest, it runs between the forest and a
wall for a short distance, then turns right through a gate near a
sheepfold and descends to Bank House Farm. When you reach the
farm, follow the access road which later turns sharply to the left
behind New House and soon joins a tarmac lane. Turn left and walk
along the lane for about a mile as far as Nab End, the first house on the
right.

When you reach the entrance drive to Nab End, continue along the
road for a short distance to reach a gate on the right into the former
farmyard, followed by a stile. Cross over the stile and follow an
enclosed path to another stile, then cross over a ditch and a stile in a
wire fence. Now turn left and walk over to a bridge over Glaisdale
Beck. Cross over this, continue slightly left of straight ahead to pass
through a gate and then head straight for a slate-roofed house called
Hutton Lodge to gain access to the road by means of a field gate to the
right of a garden plot.

Turn right and follow the road down the dale for about 2¼ miles.

31

The road forks just before Glaisdale Church and, if you take the right-hand road and then turn right at the next junction, you will eventually reach Glaisdale Station. Note that the walk can be shortened by crossing the dale from New House to the road on the far side.

Staithes and Port Mulgrave

Starting Point: Car park at the top of the steep hill on the minor road leading to the old village of Staithes, G.R. 781185.

Public Transport: United bus route X56/256 Middlesbrough-Guisborough-Loftus-Whitby operates along the A174 road. Alight at Staithes Lane End, ¼ mile south of the starting point.

Distance: 5½ miles.

START by walking down the steep road towards the sea; the road turns to the right at the bottom of the hill and passes the Cod and Lobster Inn to reach the sea front. Continue up Church Street just past the inn and, at the top of the street, keep straight on along a rough path until it levels out, and then turn left along the path in the hollow. Follow this path past a farm, then continue straight ahead across the fields, eventually turning diagonally uphill to reach the cliff edge. Turn right and walk along the cliff path to a terrace of cottages at Port Mulgrave.

Continue along the road and follow it inland as far as the telephone kiosk, then turn right along a wide unsurfaced track. At the far end, enter a field and look for a gate into a caravan site on your right, but do not go through it. Instead, turn left at the gate and follow a signposted footpath across the field, continuing along the right-hand side of a short length of hedge. Cross over a stile, follow the wire fence on your left until it turns to the left, then continue forward and descend the slope to reach another stile. Cross over this and continue to the main road, where you turn right.

Walk along the road until it makes a sharp right-hand bend, then turn left over a cattle grid and follow the farm road to Seaton Hall Farm. When you reach the farm, turn right and pass to the right of the farm buildings, then go through a gate into a field. Continue for 60 feet, then turn left and walk along the field, keeping parallel with the houses visible over on your right. Keep straight ahead, walking slightly to the left of the remains of a hedge, then drop down to a rather slippery stone step stile near the 'Fox and Hounds'.

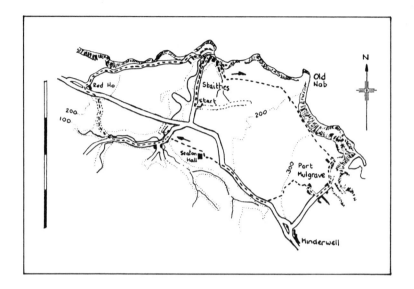

Turn left along the road, cross the bridge over Easington Beck, then turn right and follow the road which runs parallel to the beck. Continue until the road crosses a ford and starts to go uphill near a brick bungalow, then bear right on to a wide track. Cross over a bridge and follow a road uphill to reach the main A174 road. Turn left and walk along the road for a short distance, turn right on to a minor road near a farm, continuing along the road signposted 'Unsuitable for motors'. This passes the cottages at Cowbar and descends to the Roxby Beck at Staithes, which is crossed by means of a footbridge. Turn right when you reach the main street and walk uphill to your starting point.

Loftus, Handale and Roxby

Starting Point: Loftus Market Place, G.R. 723182.

Public Transport: Loftus can be reached from Whitby, Middlesbrough, Guisborough, Eston, Redcar, Marske and Saltburn by bus services operated by United.

Distance: 9½ miles.

WALK along the main road to the Town Hall clock tower, then turn left and continue past the church and down a narrow lane. At the

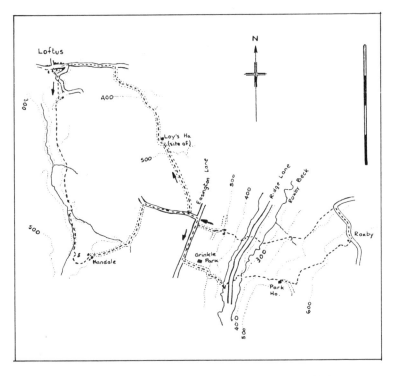

bottom, cross over the footbridge and follow the path which starts at the stone steps near the entrance drive to White Gates and crosses over the railway. When you reach a wide farm track, turn right and walk towards Rose Cottage, then cross over a stile on your left and pass to the left of the cottage. Beyond the cottage, the path turns left alongside a wire fence, then right alongside a hedge to reach a stile between two gates. Cross over this and continue along the left-hand edge of the wood ahead of you. The path descends to a footbridge and you then keep straight ahead past the left-hand edge of another wood. When its boundary turns right at an old gate, bear slightly left and walk across the hillside, then head for the point at which a wire fence comes down to the boundary of the wood.

Cross over a stile with a nearby signpost pointing to Handale, drop down through the wood and turn left at the bottom of the slope. Now walk along the left-hand side of the beck and, when you come to an embankment over the beck, bear right for a few yards and continue on the same side. At the far end of the wood, cross over a stile into rough pastureland, walk alongside the wooden fence by the beck and cross over a stile at the other end of the pasture. Turn left, continuing uphill to a wicket gate into a field, then follow the edge of a wood round to the left to reach the access road to Handale Farm. Continue forward along the road to reach a road junction about three-quarters of a mile later. Turn right and continue to another road junction, where you turn right again.

Follow the road for about half a mile and turn left along a broad lane which passes Grinkle Park Farm, then proceed downhill along a wide enclosed track, which eventually narrows to a woodland path which descends to Easington Beck and ascends to Ridge Lane. Your route continues slightly to the left on the other side of the lane. The path soon turns left and, about 40 yards later, you turn right down a stepped path which crosses over Roxby Beck and leads uphill to a stile into a field. Now walk around the left-hand side of the hillside in front of you and head for the top left-hand corner of the field, where a broad rutted track crosses a streamlet and takes you past the left-hand side of Park House. Go through the gate across the access road and follow the green road alongside the fence on your left. At the end of the fence, it turns left and is enclosed between hedges for a short distance, before bearing right across the middle of a field to reach a stile. Cross over the stile, follow the hedge on your left and climb over a fence into the next field. Continue alongside the hedge, which later swings to the right, then cross over a stile by a gate and keep straight on to reach the road near the Fox Inn at Roxby.

Turn left and walk down the road until it turns sharply to the right, then go through the second gate on the left (with a footpath sign). Do not follow the wide track, but bear left through another gate. Follow the wall on your left for two fields and continue until you are about half-way along the edge of the third field. Cross the hedge on your left and turn right along an enclosed wide track, crossing over a stile near a gate and continuing along the track, which later turns right and descends diagonally down a field. After crossing over a bridge, continue downhill and round to the left into a field and then the route is not obvious. Now turn 45 degrees to the right and walk to the far right-hand corner of the field, where there is a footbridge over Roxby Beck. Cross over this and keep straight on to reach Ridge Lane, continuing on the other side along a path which descends to Easington Beck.

Walk up the slope on the other side and, at the top of the final section of handrail, bear diagonally to the right towards the hedge. Cross over a well-hidden plank footbridge, then turn left and walk to the top left-hand corner of the field behind Spring House. Now go through the ornamental iron gate and walk through the garden, leaving the property via the entrance gate and turning left along a rough lane which takes you to Easington Lane. Turn right, then shortly afterwards turn left into another lane, which is followed for about 200 yards to the start of a wide track on the right known as Loy's Lane. Continue along it to reach the main road near Loftus cemetery, then turn left and walk back to the Market Place.

Percy Cross Rigg and Mill Bank Wood

Starting Point: Near Kildale Railway Station, G.R. 605095.

Public Transport: Kildale Station is on the Middlesbrough to Whitby railway line (no Sunday services except in summer).

Distance: 9½ miles.

FOLLOW the road from the station into Kildale village and turn left along the road to Commondale and Castleton. After about three-quarters of a mile, turn left by the letter box and continue along the lane to New Row Cottages, then keep straight on uphill along a wide track. When you reach the road over Percy Cross Rigg, turn left and walk along the road. The tarmac terminates at the end of a wood, but you should continue along the unsurfaced road for a mile to reach a gate across the road. Go through this and immediately turn left along a forest road which follows the edge of the forest.

After about half a mile, the forest road turns to the right, and soon afterwards you turn left through a wicket gate and follow a distinct path through the heather towards Roseberry Topping. A second wicket gate is reached; go through this and continue downhill, turning left through a gate at the bottom. From here a field road is followed to Airy Holme Farm, where you bear left and pass in front of the farmhouse, continuing along a tarmac lane to a crossroads near some white-painted cottages.

Go straight across at the crossroads and follow a tarmac lane, which finishes at a house called 'Cherrygarth' and then continues as a rough enclosed track. Go through the gate at the top of the hill, continuing alongside a stone wall and then keeping straight on past the left-hand side of a fence. When you reach the next gate, walk straight across the forest road on the other side and follow a narrow path

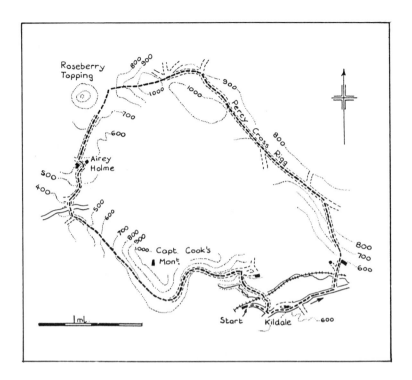

through the trees, continuing over a bracken-covered open hillside. There is a good view of the Cleveland Hills on your right as you walk along. Eventually Mill Bank Wood is entered through two old stone gateposts and, if you keep straight on, you will join a rather muddy forest track which takes you to a stile and gate, giving access to a tarmac road near Bankside Farm. Follow the road downhill to a 'T' junction at Kildale village, then turn right to reach your starting point.

Roseberry Topping and Easby Moor

Starting Point: High Green at the eastern end of High Street in the village of Great Ayton, G.R. 563106.

Public Transport: The following buses pass High Green: United services 281, Redcar-Guisborough-Stokesley; 290, Middlesbrough-Great Ayton-Stokesley.

Distance: 6½ miles

LEAVE High Green in an easterly direction (right if standing facing the shops) and follow the road round to the left towards Newton. Pass

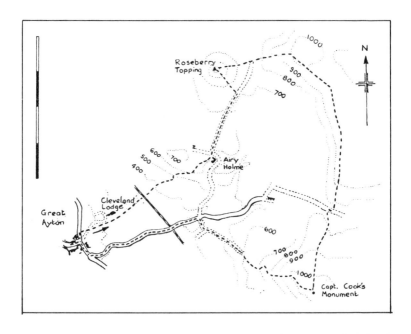

through an iron gate in the wall on the right and follow a well-defined path which passes to the right of Cleveland Lodge. Cross the railway and the access road to a lineside cottage, then continue straight ahead, eventually turning left to a stile at the edge of Cliff Ridge Wood. Ascend to an iron gate, then climb diagonally to the right along a narrow path, climb over the stile in the wire fence at the top and turn right. Follow the edge of the field, cross over another stile, walk beside the wire fence on your right and cross over a stile on the access road to Airey Holme Farm. Continue towards the farm and, just after passing the farmhouse, turn right and follow a cart track. After about 500 yards the main muddy track bears slightly to the right, but you must keep straight ahead along a wide grassy track which ascends gradually to a wicket gate at the base of Roseberry Topping. Go through this, turn left and climb to the summit.

From the summit, walk eastwards along the ridge to near the end, where you bear left and descend by an obvious path, which soon follows the left-hand side of the wall. At the bottom, keep straight on uphill and, after passing through a wicket gate in a wall, continue alongside the wall on your right. About a mile later, bear right over the minor road at Gribdale Gate and ascend by a wide forest track to Captain Cook's Monument on the summit of Easby Moor.

If you stand with your back to the inscription on the base of the monument, you will see a path going diagonally to the right. Continue along this path; after a short distance it follows a wall, and when the wall makes a right-angled bend, go diagonally to the left and enter a forest. Follow the path downhill through the forest and go through a wicket gate at the bottom. Now walk beside the wall on your right, then turn right along a track which leads to a wicket gate and then becomes an enclosed green lane. Eventually you come to a crossroads, where you turn left and follow the road to a 'T' junction on the outskirts of Green Ayton. To reach High Green, turn right and then left about 300 yards later.

Urra Moor and Botton Head

Starting Point: Car park near the summit of Clay Bank on the Stokesley-Helmsley road (B1257), G.R. 572035.

Public Transport: United bus route 294, Middlesbrough-Stokesley-Helmsley passes the starting point (Friday only).

Distance: 6 miles.

From the car park walk along the main road towards Helmsley until the road begins to descend. Go through the wicket gate on the left and follow the distinct path along the wall (signposted Cleveland Way); eventually it climbs up through a rocky cleft and then continues to a gate in a stone wall. Where the main path levels out, about 60 feet beyond the wall, turn off right along a faint path. This leads to and then continues alongside the ditch and mound of a man-made earthwork of unknown origin, which follows the edge of the moor overlooking Bilsdale.

Half a mile later the path crosses a stream and then bends back on itself on the other side. It then continues on the level still following the earthwork. As you walk on, turn round for an unusual view of Roseberry Topping and Captain Cook's Monument on Easby Moor, visible through the gap in the Cleveland Hills crossed by the main road. The hill to the left of the gap is Hasty Bank, and further left beyond it is the long ridge of Cold Moor, which extends along the opposite side of Bilsdale.

The ditch and mound disappear in boggy ground just before a stone wall is reached. Head for the wall and walk with it on your right to its

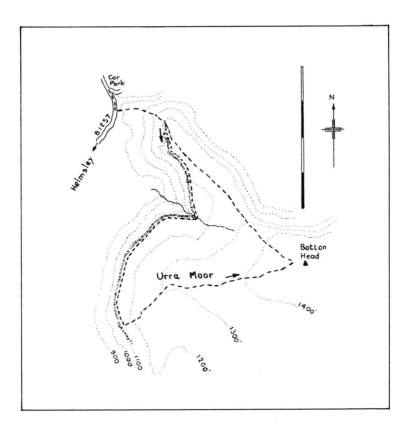

far end, where you continue walking in a straight line, eventually reaching the bridle road which has ascended from Chop Gate and Seave Green. There is a large notice board to the left, concerning the protection of moorland plants, animals and birds. Turn left here and follow the bridle road to the moor top, where another smaller signpost on the left states 'To Bloworth Crossing'. Walk along this track, which is a fire break made on the route of the path. It continues for about 1½ miles until, just beyond a large cairn on the left, it meets a track of similar size at a 'T' junction by a boundary stone.

On the moor on the opposite side of the track is a Triangulation Point on Botton Head, the highest point on the North York Moors at 1,489 feet (454 metres) above sea level. At the junction, the left turn takes you all the way back to the car park at Clay Bank.

Chop Gate, Cold Moor and Carlton Moor

Starting Point: Car park immediately to the south of Chop Gate village on the Stokesley-Helmsley road (B1257), G.R. 558993.

Distance: 10 miles.

FROM the car park walk along the road into Chop Gate village. Turn left on to the road to Carlton and then immediately to the right, continuing along the footpath in the grassy hollow which starts near the Wesleyan Chapel. This path later widens to become a grassy lane and leads eventually to a gate giving access to the open moor. Go through the gate and walk alongside the wall on the right for a short distance until you reach the end of a conifer plantation, then continue slightly left of straight ahead along a narrow path through the bracken. This path continues over heather-clad moor, then widens and ascends to the crest of Cold Moor, where it joins another wide track. Turn right along this track, and then keep walking along the top of the ridge until you reach its most northerly point, which is crossed by the very distinct Cleveland Way footpath.

Turn left along the Cleveland Way, which soon descends to a gate. Pass through it, follow the left-hand side of the wall and then go through a second gate. Now follow the wall on your left for a short distance, then climb to the top of Cringle Moor using a path which is towards the middle of the shale heaps. (An alternative path over on the right can be used to cut out the climb and rejoins the main route later. This latter path is well used but is not a designated right of way). The main path leads to a memorial seat and plaque, which points out the features of the landscape visible from this excellent viewpoint. It then descends alongside a wall, is joined by the alternative path and follows the right-hand side of a wire fence. At the end of the fence take the distinct path which passes to the right of a small plantation of trees and joins a tarmac road by a Cleveland Way sign.

Continue to the right of the forestry plantation on the opposite side of the road and then turn left along a rough-surfaced road which leads uphill to a stile and gateway at the boundary of the land belonging to the Gliding Club. After the gateway look for a line of telegraph poles on the left and, when you reach the last pole, a very narrow path branches off to the left just before the road bends to the right. Follow this path slightly uphill through the heather and, when you reach the end of a grassy glider runaway, continue on the opposite side along a

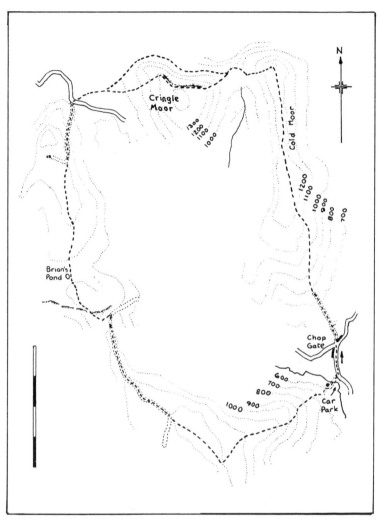

wide track. This track joins another near a rocky outcrop and by turning left you will eventually reach a small reedy pond called Brian's Pond. From the pond keep straight ahead along a wide path which later narrows and descends along the right-hand side of a hollow in the heather. The route continues to a stile and then follows the left-hand side of a wall to reach a wide grassy track, which comes through a gate in the wall.

Turn left and follow this grassy track until it starts to descend. Now turn right and a short distance later right again along a wide stony track which takes you along the ridge between Raisdale (on the left) and Scugdale. After about a mile the track swings away from Raisdale and you turn left by a wooden post along a track bulldozed through the heather. This track leads past Green Howe, a tumulus with a boundary stone on top, and later makes a sharp right turn near a similar tumulus called Cock Howe. Now walk through the heather to the right-hand side of Cock Howe and continue along the path which swings round to the right and heads downhill towards Bilsdale. The way is obvious until the ground starts to fall away steeply at the end of the ridge. It is now important not to follow the track in the hollow which swings to the right. Instead bear slightly to the left and follow a well-defined path below the end of the ridge to reach a stile from which the car park is normally visible below. Cross over the stile, follow the path down the right-hand side of the field and then walk down one of the hollow paths which lead to a wide enclosed track giving access to the rear of the car park.

Swainby, Carlton Moor and Faceby

Starting Point: Adjacent to Swainby village church, G.R. 478020.

Public Transport: Swainby is served by the following bus route: United 290/295 Middlesbrough-Stokesley-Northallerton (Monday - Saturday only)

Distance: 9½ miles.

WALK along the main street in a southerly direction towards the hills and turn left at the end of the village along Scugdale Road. Continue for about a mile to the telephone kiosk at Heathwaite, then turn left on to the broad track signposted 'Cleveland Way' and 'LWW', the abbreviation for Lyke Wake Walk. This climbs steadily uphill and passes along the bottom edge of a forest to a gap in the trees, where you turn right and ascend a flight of steps leading to open moorland. A distinct path continues along the northern edge of Live Moor and Holey Moor, ultimately reaching the triangulation pillar on the top of Carlton Moor and then descending steeply to the Chop Gate to Carlton minor road. On a clear day there are extensive views westwards to the Pennines from this section of the route.

Turn left and follow the road steeply downhill round an S-bend and over a cattle grid. About a quarter of a mile later, turn left along an

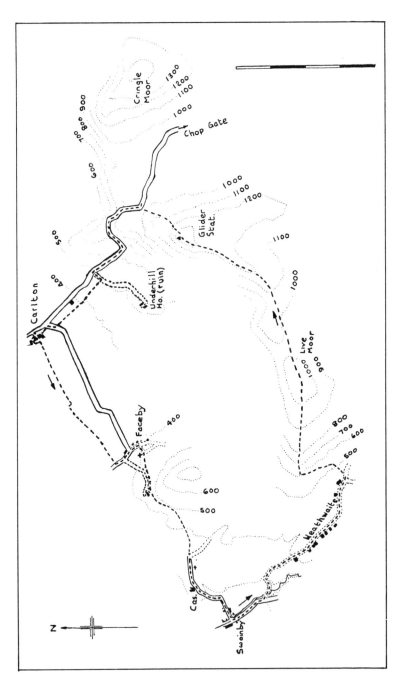

Cringle
Moor

1300
1200
1100
1000

900
800

Chop Gate

700

600

1000
1100
1200

Glider
Stat.

1100

500

400

1000
900

Carlton

Underhill
Ho. (ruin)

Live
Moor

1000
900

Faceby

400

800
700
600

600

500

500

600

Heathwaite

Cas.

Swainby

N

44

unsurfaced farm road which has a stone pillar on each side, then go through a gate. There is a hedge on your right and, when this turns right, you must also turn right and walk down towards Carlton village, keeping alongside the hedge. The hedge changes to a wire fence and, when this turns right, continue in a forward direction to reach a road near a red-roofed stone cottage. Turn right and walk along the road for a short distance, then turn left along a tarmac path which starts near a seat and leads to the end of one of the roads through Carlton village. Ignore the road which bears right over a ford, and keep straight ahead through the village.

A short distance later, a footpath sign points to a gap in the houses opposite a cobbled path leading down to a footbridge on your right. Turn left, enter a field by means of a stile near a gate and walk alongside the hedge on your left to reach a footbridge. Cross over this, turn left along the ditch, then turn right and follow the hedge to the far end of a large field. Continue straight ahead, passing to the right of two electricity poles in the next field, crossing over a footbridge and eventually reaching the road at Faceby.

Turn left and walk as far as 'The Sutton Arms', continuing along the road signposted 'Faceby Only'. The next lane on the right leads to Faceby Church and terminates at the adjacent cottage, where you turn left and go through a stone squeezer stile into a field. Walk diagonally to the right towards a poultry farm, cross over a stile and continue along the edge of a wood, cross over two stiles in succession near a stone-built bungalow. Keep straight on along a wide grassy track, cross over the stile near the gate at the end and continue alongside the hedge on your left. As you approach the next gate, look for a stile on your right; cross over this into the field below and continue along the hedgeside, making for Whorlton Church. The path is now fairly obvious and leads to a right-angled bend in a lane, where you bear right and return to Swainby by following the lane past the church, which is worth a visit, and the remains of Whorlton Castle.

Black Hambleton

Starting Point: On the minor road between Osmotherley and Hawnby, 2 miles from Osmotherley on the top of the moors where the road makes a left-hand right-angled bend before descending into Ryedale, G.R. 479959.

Distance: 9 miles.

WALK southwards along the wide rough-surfaced track, which starts at the bend in the road and heads towards the prominent hill called Black Hambleton. This former cattle drovers' road is part of the Cleveland Way. When you reach a gate in the forest fence, the drovers' road continues outside the fence and soon afterwards there is another gate at the edge of the forest and a sign stating 'Bridleway to Nether Silton'. Cross over the nearby stile and follow the forest path to its junction with a black unmetalled forest road. Turn left and keep straight ahead; after about a mile the road leaves the forest by a gate near a cattle grid.

Approximately half-way between this gate and the farm visible on the right (Hunter's Hill) the road passes over a stream, about 50 yards beyond which there is a caravan on the left. Go through the nearby gate, continue straight ahead and pass through a gate to the right of a row of trees and then another gate in the hedgerow ahead of you. Now follow the field boundary round to your right, where you go through the gate which has concrete gateposts. Walk to the far end of the field, turn right for a short distance until just before you reach a row of trees and then cross over the stile on your left to gain access to the field next to Honeykiln Farm. From here the right of way should go to the far left-hand corner of the field, but there is no way out; instead walk diagonally across the field to near the far right-hand corner, where you gain access to the farm track serving Honeykiln Farm by means of a hurdle, where there used to be a waymarked stile.

Walk away from the farm and turn left towards Thwaites Farm for a short distance. About 15 feet before the farm gate, cross over the fence on the right and walk down the hedgrow on your left and pass through the gate at the bottom corner of the field. Continue downhill to another gate at the left-hand corner of the next field. After passing through this gate, keep to the left of the field and cross over the barbed wire fence at the bottom. Head across the last field to a white gate which gives access to the lane leading from Nether Silton to Kepwick.

Turn left and follow the lane for about quarter of a mile until you reach a stone house on the left. Leave the road immediately before this

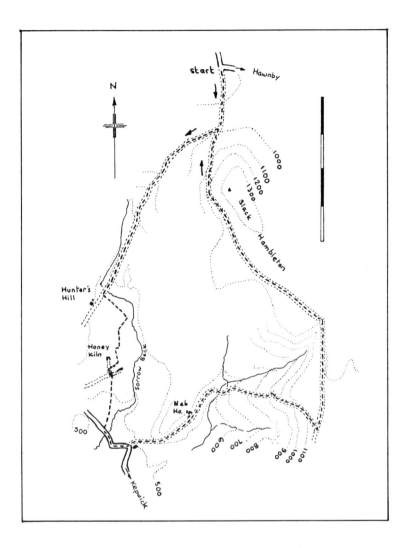

house and follow the wide track leading to Nab Farm. When you approach the farm, continue along the concrete road which takes you past the right-hand side of all the farm buidings. On the other side, follow a wide track across grassland, then cross over a stream and bear left towards a gate near an old limekiln. The track then goes across open country to a wall, which is followed to the top of the hill where there is a gate giving access to a broad track enclosed between stone walls. As you ascend, note the rocks on the hillside on the left — Whitestone Scar.

47

It is worthwhile to pause at the top and look back to where you have come from. Immediately below is Nab Farm, almost looking like a miniature doll's house, and beyond it the Vale of Mowbray is spread like a carpet to the Yorkshire Dales and Pennines. Wensleydale is the prominent dale in front of you on the horizon, and the distinctive peak immediately to the left of it is Penhill.

Turn left after passing through the gate and continue along the grassy track, which is part of the drovers' road and the Cleveland Way. After about three-quarters of a mile it turns to the left, then proceeds along the western side of Black Hambleton, before descending to take you back to your starting point. As you approach the finish, note Osmotherley village and church behind some small reservoirs slightly to the left of you.

Paradise

Starting Point: On the minor road from Boltby to Hawnby, 1 mile from Boltby, 25 yards up Sneck Yate Bank where a well-defined forestry track goes off to the left and there is a wide enough open space to park your car, G.R. 503872.

Distance: 6 miles (full route); 5 miles (shorter route).

GO through the gate, by which you have parked your car, and follow the forestry track, passing a reservoir over to your right after about one mile. Proceed straight on along the track, then bear right at the next two junctions. Bear left at the third junction and follow a forest track which goes uphill. At the top of the hill, where the track turns sharply to the left, turn right along a short section of track barred to vehicular access. Walk round either end of the barrier at the top and continue uphill along the sloping forest track opposite the barrier.

At the top of the hill turn left on to a wide track, then immediately to the right on to a broad grassy forest track, which leads to the old cattle drovers' road at the far end, where you turn right. Continue along the unmetalled drovers' road, passing through a gate at the end of the forest to reach a gate on the right-hand side signposted 'Cleveland Way'. Pass through this gate and proceed to High Paradise Farm. On the far side of the farm, continue along the tarmac access road which descends through woodland and leads to a gate about 500 yards from the farm. The road then turns sharply to the right, but you must keep

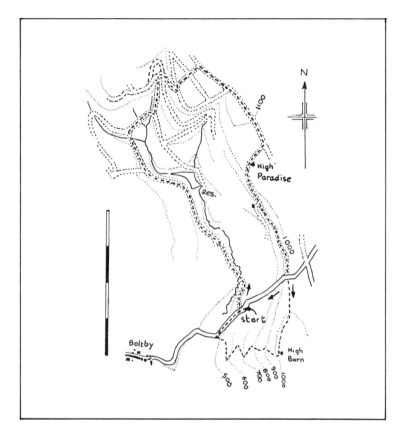

straight ahead along a broad grassy track (signposted 'Cleveland Way') which goes through woodland to reach the tarmac road near the top of Sneck Yate Bank.

If you wish to follow the shorter route, descend the bank back to your car. Otherwise cross the road and follow a broad track to High Barn at the top of the hill, where you turn sharply to the right opposite the gate just past the farm building. A broad grassy track goes through a gap in the trees, descends in a slight hollow, bends to the left above a wall and takes you to a gate in a wire fence. Go through the gate, walk to the far right-hand corner of the field, where you turn left along a sunken track bordered by trees and bushes on the downhill side. Turn right when you reach a wire fence and follow the fence down to a broad stony forestry access track. Turn right along this track and follow it to the tarmac road, where you turn right to reach the start of the walk about a quarter of a mile later.

White Horse of Kilburn

Starting Point: Car park at the summit of Sutton Bank on the Thirsk-Helmsley road (A170), 4 miles from Thirsk, G.R. 514830.

Distance: 6½ miles.

FINE views westwards across the Vale of York to the Yorkshire Dales and the Pennines are obtained during this walk, which is one of the most varied in the National Park.

From the car park, cross over the main road and follow the footpath which begins almost opposite the junction with the by-road to Cold Kirby and Old Byland. The path leads to a viewpoint indicator and then continues along the edge of the edge of the steep escarpment for 1¼ miles. At the end of the path you will reach the White Horse of Kilburn, identifiable at this stage only as a large white area immediately below on the right, from which both turf and vegetation have been cleared. Directly beyond this, descend the hillside by a series of steps to a car park clearly visible below on the right.

Continue descending the hillside, either by a series of hairpin bends in the minor road, or by a path which follows the left-hand side of the road, until you reach a steep hill sign. About 50 yards beyond this, follow the farm road branching off to the right and, where it turns left to Acre House Farm, keep straight on along a grassy track between hedges, ultimately entering a forestry plantation. Follow the track through the Forestry Commission land until the main access track comes in from the right.

Keep straight on along this track to take the left fork at the bottom of the hill. Your way winds round the side of Hood Hill and, as the path bears left, a field and boundary fence are immediately on your right. As soon as the boundary fence moves away from the track, follow the fence downhill to pass through a wicket gate into a field. Walk down the field towards Hood Grange (the ancient stone farmhouse, a quarter of a mile away in the valley bottom). Just before you reach the farm, turn left along the side of the beck for a short distance, then cross over a footbridge and walk alongside a wire fence to reach the farm access road. Turn left along the road, and follow it round a right and left-hand bend until the main Thirsk-Helmsley road is reached.

Turn sharp right along the main road, and at the top of a short incline after about 100 yards, turn left to follow the access road to Cleaves Farm. On reaching the farm buildings, pass through the gate

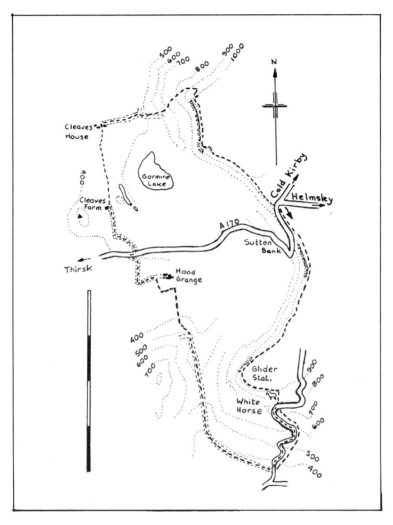

in front of you and follow the rough track across the field and then go through another gate. In front of you will be seen a third gate. Do not go through this, but bear slightly to the left, and follow the hedge towards a fourth gate between some trees. The way is now clear to Cleaves Farm in front of you. On reaching the boundary of the property, turn right over a stile by a gate and then immediately left. Continue along the edge of the grounds to reach a minor road.

Turn right along the road, and after a quarter of a mile Southwood Lodge with an elegantly cut hawthorn tree is reached on the left.

51

Immediately after passing the cottage, bear slightly right along the 'Bridlepath to Gormire'. After about 100 yards from the cottage, a narrower path will be seen bearing left as the main path bears right. It is signposted 'Thirlby Bank' on a small ground-level sign, which may be obscured by bracken in summer. Follow it gradually uphill; it is signposted periodically. At the highest point the Cleveland Way is joined as it follows the escarpment edge from Sneck Yate Bank to Sutton Bank. Turn right, and in three quarters of a mile you will have returned to the car park from which you have started.

Rievaulx and Old Byland

Starting Point: Rievaulx, 3 miles north-east of Helmsley, G.R. 575850. Note: the abbey car park is for visitors only. Park in a small inconspicuous parking place by the riverside about 400 yards south of the village.

Distance: 8½ miles.

START by walking away from the village along the road beside the River Rye. When you reach a 'T' junction, turn right over the bridge towards Scawton and continue straight ahead for about one mile. Just after the road bends sharply to the left, turn right into a wide entrance signposted 'Cleveland Way', then go through the gate and follow the forestry road along the edge of the woods past three large ponds. Rievaulx Forest is entered through a gate, then the road swings round to the right and becomes the obvious main way up the valley (paths up side valleys to the left should be ignored, including the Cleveland Way).

After about 1½ miles you reach a tarmac road and turn right to follow it to Old Byland. Pass through the village and turn left towards Hawnby and then right at the next junction. Continue straight on along the road with an 'Unsuitable for Motor Vehicles' sign. After bending sharply to the left, the road descends steeply and is followed as far as some tall pine trees on the right. Just before these, turn right through a gate and continue along the track beside the remains of a wall above Caydale Mill. Look for a bridleway sign on your right and, when you reach it, walk along the hillside in the direction indicated by the sign, keeping parallel to the beck. Another bridleway sign is passed, then you go through the gate ahead of you and continue along

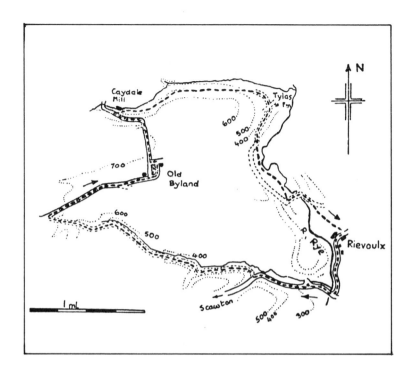

a wide track through woodland, emerging into open country near Tylas Farm.

Now follow the tarmac road away from the farm until it drops down steeply to a small stream, on the other side of which there is a gate on the left. Go through this, cross the field to the riverside and walk downstream along what soon becomes a narrow woodland path along the bank of the River Rye. After crossing the stile out of the wood, keep straight on to reach a rough-surfaced lane. Turn left along the lane, cross over Bow Bridge and continue until the large trees on the right are reached. Cross over the nearby stile, continue along the riverside and further on cross over two stiles which are close together. Now head straight for Rievaulx Abbey, keeping to the right of a wire fence and continuing along a short length of enclosed green lane. The road through Rievaulx is joined by passing through two gates in succession on the right-hand side of a stone outbuilding. Turn right to reach your starting point.

Roppa Edge

Starting Point: Entrance to the Forestry Commission picnic place near the summit of Newgate Bank on the east side of the B1257 Stokesley to Helmsley road (4½ miles north-west of Helmsley), G.R. 563888. Car parking at the picnic place.

Distance: 10 miles.

START the walk by following the track which is signposted 'Footpath to Cow House Bank' at the main road. This track carries straight on as a wide track through the forest when the access road to the picnic place swings sharply to the left. Half a mile later you emerge on to the open moor and the views are now magnificent; over on the left is the long ridge of Easterside Hill at the junction of Rydale and Bilsdale, whilst over on the right is the Vale of Pickering with the Howardian Hills beyond it. Eventually the ordance point on the summit of the moor is reached and from this point, not only is there an excellent view of much of the western section of the North York Moors, but Buckden Pike and Great Whernside are clearly visible in the far west.

From the summit continue along the track and, where it swings to the right opposite the sculpture, cross over a stile and continue straight ahead on the opposite side of the tarmac road along the track which follows the edge of the forest. After 1½ miles you cross over a stile adjacent to a barrier and, immediately on the left, is a memorial seat worthy of a diversion for the fine view northwards. After a short distance the track reaches the Helmsley to Bransdale road, where you turn left and walk along the road.

The road descends to a stream and about 250 yards later there is a wide track on the left signposted 'Public Footpath'. Turn left here and follow the track as it goes through a gate, crosses a ford and climbs up to a second gate at the edge of dense forest. On the other side of this, follow the main track round to the left as far as the next junction, where you keep straight ahead along a lesser track and forsake the main track, which turns left and descends. Proceed straight ahead as far as a horseshoe bend in a forest road near the far end of the forest, where you take the right-hand track. When you reach a field, turn right and follow the forest road outside the field, then turn left and continue along the forest road to its junction with another forest road. Now go through the gate on your left and follow a broad track towards Snaper House. A little further on, where the track turns left through a gate towards the farm buildings, bear right and enter the next field.

Continue parallel to the wall on your left until, after a short

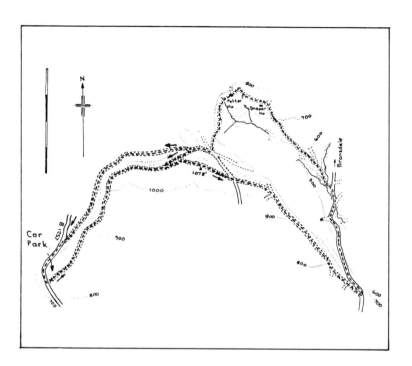

distance, it turns slightly to the left. At this point, diverge away from it
and follow an indistinct broad track through the bracken, passing
about 60 feet to the right of a holly tree and to the right of two large
piles of stones. A broad path continues straight ahead through the
bracken and takes you to a bridge over a ditch near a gate in a stone
wall. Go through the gate, cross the field to the farm (Potter House)
and enter the farmyard via a gate to the left of the farmhouse. Now
walk round to the right and follow the farm road away from the farm.
Continue as far as a crossroads in the forest, identified by a footpath
signpost, and then turn right on to a forest road.

When you reach a gateway at the edge of the forest, there is a choice
of routes. A track on the left goes diagonally on to the top of Roppa
Edge and joins the outward track. Turn right at the top to reach your
starting point. Alternatively, continue along the forest road to reach
the Stokesley to Helmsley road, then turn left and walk up the hill to
the car park.